HOW GRACE WILL TAKE YOUR
BUSINESS WHERE GRINDING CAN'T

SHAE BYNES

Grace Over Grind: How Grace Will Take Your Business Where Grinding Can't

Published by Kingdom Driven Publishing
4846 N. University Drive #406 | Lauderhill, FL, 33351 USA

KingdomDrivenEntrepreneur.com

Interior Design | Cover Design
DHBonner Virtual Solutions LLC
www.dhbonner.net

Published in the United States of America

Scripture unless otherwise indicated taken from the Holy Bible, NEW INTERNATIONAL VERSION ®, NIV ® Copyright © 1973, 1978, 1984, 2011 by Biblica, Inc. ® Used by permission. All rights reserved worldwide.

ISBN for paperback: 978-0-9896322-9-4
ISBN for hardcover: 978-0-9996763-0-1

This book is dedicated to my beautiful daughters

Anisa Rachelle (forever my rock)
Nia Morgan (forever my love bug)
Malia Grace (forever my grace baby)

I love you all to infinity (plus one)

PRAISE FOR GRACE OVER GRIND

"Eloquent without excess. Spot on in truth, application, and insight. The revelation Shae shares in *Grace Over Grind* is your prescription to transform your sweat-equity into kingdom-equity without pain.

This is more than a must-read - it is a must-revisit-often entrepreneurial classic for kingdom-driven marketplace warriors."

Dr. Jim Harris
Advisor to leaders & award-winning author of
*Our Unfair Advantage: Unleash the Power of
Holy Spirit in Your Business*

***

"If you can read one book this year, it should be *Grace over Grind*! This amazing tool will teach you how to stop grinding your way to success and instead show you how to partner with God. You will ultimately accomplish more than you could ask or imagine!"

Kelly Thorne Gore
iBloom Founder & President

"In *Grace Over Grind*, Shae Bynes gives voice to that feeling so many Christian entrepreneurs I work with have privately shared: all this "grinding and hustling" doesn't seem like it fits with God's plan for my life. The truth is, it's not at all right.

In this book, you'll find a better way, inspired by scripture and testimony, along with signs you've been doing it wrong and simple steps to improve, starting today, complete with exercises to help you pray, think, and act in accordance with the plan God has for your business and your life.
It's time to stop grinding and start building your business with grace and peace."

Felicia J. Slattery, M.A., M.Ad.Ed.
Best-Selling Author of *Kill the Elevator Speech: Stop Selling, Start Connecting*,
and *The REAL Relationship Challenger: Creating Connections in an Overly-Connected World*

***

"Business is not for the faint-hearted. Many businesses fail in the first three years. You have to give it at least 100% to even survive the start! So how can you survive, let alone succeed without grinding yourself to the floor? Where is God in all of this? Is there an advantage to working with God? In *Grace Over Grind*, Shae Bynes gives us a timeless but mostly ignored key to accessing more.

This book will provoke and position you to leverage the limitless support of Heaven in your pursuit of building a business and life that thrives in every respect. I dare you to live this life as God intended and stand out from those around you by the peace and performance that can only come from an intimacy of the Founding Creating Entrepreneur of the Universe."

Andy Mason
Director of Heaven in Business
Author of *God With You at Work*

***

"*Grace over Grind* is a must read for all entrepreneurs of faith. Shae masterfully lays out this spiritual concept with well-selected examples to reinforce your learning. If you are tired of the struggle in your business and ready to receive success through the sweatless anointing of God's grace, then consume every page in this powerful book and apply it to your business."

Amos Johnson Jr., Ph.D.
Founder of Church for Entrepreneurs
Author of *Take Control of Your Financial Destiny:
9 Christian Entrepreneurship Principles to
Developing a God-Inspired Business*

TABLE OF CONTENTS

ACKNOWLEDGMENTS

There are a number of people who contributed in some way to this book being in your hands right now, and I'd like to take a moment to thank them.

Thank you Paul Wilson Jr. for the multiple conversations we had on The Kingdom Driven Entrepreneur Podcast years ago that planted the seed for the message in these pages.

Thank you to my family of mentees in our Igniters Mentoring Program for frequently asking me when I was going to write and publish this book. Not only did your enthusiasm keep me accountable to complete it, but your overall reception to this message and your commitment to live it out, has been and will continue to be such a powerful example to others!

Thank you Desireé Harris-Bonner for your brilliant work, and for helping me to express my heart in written form even more effectively.

Thank you Phil Bynes for always encouraging me to pursue all that God has destined for me. Without your support, this book (and so much more) simply would not happen.

INTRODUCTION

"Too many believers in business idolize hard work. They exalt hard work over the presence of God in business."

These are the words that Holy Spirit shared with me one day as I was at the beach, enjoying the sight of my girls laughing together as we waited for our family photographer to arrive. Two simple statements from my favorite Teacher, packed with profound and convicting truth.

In the world of entrepreneurship, *hustle and grind* is a celebrated way of life. Some of the expressions you'll commonly hear or read on t-shirts, mugs, and social media memes are "I'm on my grind", "Rise and grind!" ,"Team No Sleep", "I'll sleep when I'm dead", "I hustle hard", "Good things come to those who grind"...

The list goes on.

You may even use some of these expressions yourself presently or perhaps you did in the past. There's no condemnation or judgment here. I used to run a website with a tagline that included the phrase "get your hustle on."

Needless to say, I get it.

Well-meaning Christians have modified the idea of hustle and grind to make it more Jesus-friendly which has led to phrases such as:

Pray. Grind. Repeat.

Wake. Pray. Grind.

Eat. Pray. Hustle.

Hustle for Jesus.

God. Goals. Grind.

Grinding for God.

Push. Pray. Grind.

The phrases are different, and they sound more spiritual, but the prevailing mindset is the same.

When you look up the definition of grind in the dictionary, it is defined as *requiring much exertion* and *excessive hard work*. Synonyms for grind include the words struggle, attempt, and strain. When you look up the definition of hustle, it is defined as *making strenuous efforts to obtain especially money or business.* This should not be your testimony, and quite frankly, it doesn't have to be.

You may be thinking to yourself "Come on Shae, these are just words... it's just an expression!" But the cost of a hustle and grind mindset (even if you pray first or say you're doing it for Jesus) is simply too great for Kingdom-driven entrepreneurs. There is a supernatural realm that many Christian business owners are failing to tap into because they are busy grinding; running fast and furious to accomplish as much as possible, as quickly as possible.

This is not God's best, and if your heart is to see the realities of the Kingdom in your business, your industry, your city or even the nations, it's imperative that you create and maintain a lifestyle of working by God's grace rather than by your grind.

Consider the words on the following pages to be an invitation from Abba, your Heavenly Father, the Ultimate CEO, and best business partner you will ever have.

It's an invitation to live and work by the grace that He has so lovingly provided for you to experience His best in your business. Notice that I didn't say your best, but rather *His* best. I'm talking about the Ephesians 3:20 kind of best; which is immeasurably more than all you can ask or imagine according to His power that is at work within you.

My prayer is that this book will either serve as confirmation of what God has already placed on your heart, while helping you to grow on the path you're already on, or that it will provide you with new revelation; igniting faith and action for a different lifestyle of doing business.

Let's begin!

4 | P a g e

1

GOD'S EMPOWERING GRACE

I have good news for you (if you choose to believe it).

You don't have to strive endlessly to make things happen with the dream God placed on your heart for your business. You simply need God's empowering presence, and everything else is going to flow from there.

Grace is that empowerment. It enables you to successfully do what God has called you to do and to do what you could never do on your own. It's by God's grace that you are able to do extraordinary things, have supernatural results, and eternal impact through your business.

You are not only saved, forgiven, and transformed by grace, but you are also sustained by it. I love how the Gospel of John speaks about grace. John 1:16 refers to "grace upon grace" which is a constant and overflowing gift out of the abundance of Christ that we have received to live and to work.

I'm going to share something personal with you that on the surface may seem like it has nothing to do with business, but it's a powerful illustration of how God's grace produces supernatural results.

I'll connect the dots after I share the story.

Shortly after my 40th birthday, I gave birth to my third daughter Malia Grace. During my pregnancy, a friend of mine sent me a book called *Supernatural Childbirth* as a gift because he said that what was in that book led to his wife having two pain-free labors and sweatless deliveries of their sons.

Sounded good to me!

Ultimately I wanted a safe delivery and a healthy baby, but I was feeling the nudge from Holy Spirit to activate my faith in this area. Every time we accept an invitation from God, we have the opportunity to grow in intimacy with Him, experience His goodness in tangible ways, and allow our testimonies to bring Him glory and inspire others.

I read the book multiple times and purchased an audio called *Childbirth in the Glory* with scripture-based faith declarations that I meditated on and spoke over my child and the birth process while traveling in my car. I didn't share my supernatural birth plan with many people - not even my midwife - because frankly I knew it sounded crazy and I didn't want anyone to intentionally or unintentionally create any doubts or speak against what I was standing in faith for.

While my birth plan was to have my midwife deliver our baby at the local birthing center, things didn't go according to my plan. My body wouldn't fully cooperate and my labor stalled. Despite the stalled labor, I remained hopeful. I could feel some pressure, but I wasn't experiencing pain; even when my contractions were three to five minutes apart for over an hour. My husband and I were playing a card game between my contractions!

Things changed when my midwife told me that I was not progressing as she'd hoped and I was at a higher risk of infection due to my water breaking hours earlier. She said I'd need to go to the hospital and have the nurse administer Pitocin to help me reach the finish line.

Honestly, I was worried. I had a history of a Pitocin-induced labor with my second child, and those contractions were no joke! There was nothing natural about the frequency, length, and intensity of those contractions. I'll spare you the details of that labor process, but overall I had very unpleasant memories and was concerned about having to experience that all over again.

On the way to the hospital, I called a close friend and shared my fears with her. She reminded me of one simple truth by asking me "Is God bigger than Pitocin?" Of course, I replied "yes," and she said, "What you were believing for at the birth center, you can still experience in the hospital, even with an induced labor." She was right, and I decided to keep my faith engaged.

When I finally arrived in the hospital delivery room, the nurse started the Pitocin. About twenty minutes later, I could feel the contractions coming in stronger, but I focused my attention on the love of Jesus and the faithfulness of God, and at times would ask my husband Phil to apply counter-pressure to my lower back.

All was well.

I experienced some pressure, yet no pain.

After a few hours of contractions, I asked the nurse midwife when she was going to check to see how far I'd progressed in labor. She told me that they didn't plan to check until I was at the point where I was having difficulty managing the contractions. While I understood the infection risks, I needed to know that I was finally progressing and it didn't look like anyone was going to confirm that for me. I had no plans to pretend that the contractions were painful when they hadn't been.

I looked at the clock, and it was after 10 pm. My calm demeanor took a turn for the worst, and I suddenly became mentally, physically, and emotionally fatigued. One of my best friends is a nurse at the hospital and was with me that evening after her shift ended.

She looked at me and told me that I was built to do this, I was going to be fine, and that I needed to sit back in the bed and get some rest.

"Rest?!? Is she crazy?" I thought to myself.

I told her that I don't handle contractions well while sitting in the bed; I had tried a few positions, and I just couldn't get comfortable. I needed to be moving around.

I told her that it was late and all I wanted to know was if I was progressing because I'm physically exhausted from the past 48 hours of off and on labor and little sleep. I cried in frustration, and the last thing I wanted to do was get back in that insanely uncomfortable bed.

Eventually, I stopped arguing with my friend and laid back on the bed to supposedly "rest."

In that moment of surrender when I had absolutely nothing left to offer other than to rest, Heaven invaded the labor and delivery room. The best way to describe what happened when I lay back on that bed to rest is to say that Jesus took the wheel. Without any medication, I was suddenly in a meditative state, where I could not feel a thing - not even the pressure I was feeling earlier.

My eyes were closed and it was as if I was sleeping, but I could occasionally hear the conversation between my friend and husband about how long and strong the contractions were (they were watching the monitors) and how well I was handling them.

They later told me that for well over an hour, during the most intense parts of the labor, they would hear an occasional short and soft moan from me. The next thing I recall was hearing the nurse tell me that I was nine centimeters dilated.

After that, I was back in the meditative state, and my husband said that I moved to sit on the side of the bed; making absolutely no sound at all for the next several contractions. He asked the nurse if she turned off the Pitocin and she said "no" and that she had actually increased the levels.

The next thing I remember is waking up and telling my friend that the baby was coming. With only one push from me, and two pain-free contractions moving the baby along, our Malia Grace made her entrance into the world.

We call her our grace baby.

My girlfriend says she has never seen anything like what happened with me in that labor room. She shared that it was such a blessing to her to be a part of such a "God moment" and said, "I would never have believed someone could have given birth with such grace and favor if I hadn't seen it with my own eyes."

Holy Spirit taught and confirmed so much for me through this experience. My labor was long, and I experienced feelings of pressure, but there was no pain. Whenever the contractions strengthened and increased in frequency, I focused my attention on Jesus and experienced peace. When I had to go to the hospital, and I became exhausted because the labor was taking so long, frustration and anxiety showed up... but when I decided to rest, His supernatural abilities rested upon me.

Throughout the entire time of my resting in Him, others witnessed the increased intensity of my circumstances with the Pitocin-induced contractions. This should have been a time when the pain was so excruciating that I'd need to ask for an epidural or at least medication to dull the pain, yet it was as if I was protected in a bubble; completely surrounded by His favor. Those who witnessed it were in awe, and I was able to give birth successfully.

God was truly my dwelling place.

This is what is not only possible, but what should be a way of life for entrepreneurs in the Kingdom. Instead of having painful and strenuous labor (grind), you can rest in the empowering presence of God (grace) as you labor (work) so that you are positioned for His supernatural ability which causes you to birth the ideas on your heart in a way that brings you extraordinary success, astonishes others, and gives glory to Him.

Are You Working By Grind?

Grinding is such a prevalent way of doing business that you may not even be aware when you're relying solely upon your own strength. At times it's obvious, but other times it's wearing a mask easily mistaken for something else. At times the grinding is physical exertion, and other times it is mental (or what I call "grinding in your head"). Let's explore some of the signs that you may be working by grind.

Financial Anxiety: Considering that the survival of a business is connected with the ability to eventually create, sustain, and grow revenues and profitability, a healthy focus on the numbers is important and a principle of good stewardship. However, you're experiencing financial anxiety if you're feeling desperate about money, or your thoughts are constantly consumed by how much money you are making (or not making) in your business.

Prayerlessness: Complete prayerlessness is unlikely, but you may not be communing with God (the Ultimate CEO and business partner who is the source of your success) regularly. Your prayers are infrequent or rushed, and you're missing an essential fuel for your faith.

Lack of Sleep: Included in the Kingdom-driven entrepreneurship journey is the occasional all-nighter, but habitual sleeplessness is a sign of working by grind. A more obvious sign is lack of sleep due to stress, but a less obvious sign is when you're not sleeping because you're excited about the work that you do and simply won't stop working or you're constantly dissatisfied with the amount of time you have available to work.

Analysis Paralysis: You may feel confused, overwhelmed, and unable to move forward in your business due to frequent over-thinking and continuous analyzing. You may feel like you received direction from Holy Spirit, but fear of failure leads to immobility and asking God for endless confirmations.

No Boundaries: You make yourself available to your clients 24 hours a day, 7 days a week and keep your smartphone close at all times. You may even have fears that your ability to be successful in business is threatened by the time you need to spend with your loved ones.

No Joy or Peace: You're tired, worn-out, agitated, and carrying the stress of the everyday ups and downs of your business.

Those are the more recognizable signs, but here are some that are sneakier and perhaps may even surprise you.

For example:

- You're motivated by proving your haters and naysayers wrong
- You're motivated by the idea of sustaining yourself because "If it's going to be, it's up to me!"
- You're constantly attending networking events and conferences and/or looking for new ones to attend
- You are running two or more businesses and looking to add more for multiple streams of income even though none of your existing ones are generating a profit
- You change the customer focus God initially gave you to exclusively serve high-end clients
- You're launching new products and services that are not in alignment with the mission or vision of your business

To be clear, these are examples that can serve as signs, but it's not an all-inclusive list, nor am I saying that each of these examples is a 100% guaranteed sign of grinding. If you felt yourself feeling defensive about any of these, I want you to set that aside for now and allow Holy Spirit to speak to your heart; revealing what you need to hear from Him through what I have shared.

APPLICATION: ASK HOLY SPIRIT

Take a few minutes and ask Holy Spirit the following question and then write down the answer you receive:

In what ways am I currently grinding in business and relying upon my own strength?

You may have identified only one or two ways that you're relying on your strength, or perhaps you've identified several. Either way, there's something infinitely greater for you in store.

In the next chapters, we're going to explore the supernatural benefits of grace in your business, so that you can place hustle and grind at the feet of Jesus, and receive His best.

2

RHYTHM & REST

In Matthew 11:28-30, the scripture says that Jesus offers us a life in Him and led by Him, in exchange for the heavy burden of guilt, shame, and religious legalism. He offers us rest for our souls and a new kingdom of righteousness, peace, and joy in the Holy Spirit.

I'll never forget the first time I heard my pastor share *The Message* translation of Matthew 11:28-30 during a sermon. I was familiar with the language of Jesus saying that his yoke was easy and his burden was light; however, *The Message* translation provided another layer of insight about the gift of God's grace.

It says:

"Are you tired? Worn out? Burned out on religion? Come to me. Get away with me and you'll recover your life. I'll show you how to take a real rest. Walk with me and work with me—watch how I do it. Learn the unforced rhythms of grace. I won't lay anything heavy or ill-fitting on you. Keep company with me and you'll learn to live freely and lightly."

The sermon had nothing to do with business, but Holy Spirit immediately illuminated the connection to business for me, and it became a key "work verse" for me; much like people have life verses that serve as a personal and frequently referred to scripture.

Think of this scripture from a business context. If you're tired and worn out, it means that you're working in your own strength, versus allowing God's strength to be made perfect in your weakness in your business. Jesus provides you with this offer... keep company with Him through your life and work, and He will be your teacher and show you how to work from rest (freely and lightly) in an unforced rhythm of grace.

Rhythm comes from the Greek word *rhythmos,* which means measured flow or movement. If the rhythm is unforced, this simply means it is not forced or imposed, but rather it is a natural flow... and since this is God's grace we're talking about, it's a supernatural flow!

In short, when you keep company (abide) with Jesus, He will teach you how to flow supernaturally in your business.

That's one of the beautiful gifts of grace!

If keeping company, or abiding, with Jesus is the prerequisite for learning how to flow supernaturally in your business, the next question should be "How do I keep company and abide with Jesus?"

The answer lies in intimacy with Him. It's keeping a line of two-way conversation going, allowing Him to speak to you through His Word and by Holy Spirit. The answer also lies in working from His rest.

When we're talking about God's rest, we're not talking about the definitions you'll find in the dictionary. We're not talking about a need for refreshing physical relaxation, a vacation, or a period of inactivity.

Rest is an awareness.

It is an ongoing awareness of the presence of an unchanging and all-powerful God in your life. It is not something you strive for. Because rest is an awareness of God's presence, it's simply something that you realize and awaken to.

Rest is not something that you acquire, but something that you access, and it resides on the inside of you because you are one with Christ and there's no distance between you (see John 15:4 and Colossians 1:27 for proof)!

APPLICATION: ASK HOLY SPIRIT

Take a moment and ask Holy Spirit the following question and then write down the answer you receive:

How can things be different in my business if I consistently partner with the supernatural flow provided to me by God's grace?

Working in Rhythm and Rest

Working in the supernatural flow and rest of God looks different for everyone because your business, your spiritual DNA, and your relationship with God are uniquely yours and His directions to you will be tailor-made for you.

Because of that, it's difficult to provide a precise how-to guide; nevertheless, there are guiding principles that will help you discover your personal path to maintaining a supernatural flow with Him.

Meet with God Regularly

The most important meetings you can have in your business are the ones you have with God. It's not about having a dry religious routine, but rather about cultivating and maintaining intimacy with the Father, with Jesus, the Lover of your Soul, and with Holy Spirit.

The length of the meeting time and how you spend the meeting is completely up to you, but know that whatever time you make available will be time well spent.

Giving Him the first fruits of your work day (i.e., time before you do any work at all) is transformational, and it's worth getting up earlier than usual in order to make yourself available during the still and quiet times in the morning. Avoid the distractions of early morning television, social media, or email so that you can meditate on the goodness of God and hear from Him.

One of the entrepreneurs I've had the pleasure of mentoring is Tiffany Elder, CEO of Kingdom Culture Consulting. She shared with me that Holy Spirit taught her the importance of giving God gratitude before giving Him her business plans. Instead of first submitting her plans to God and asking Him to bless them, one day she sat before Him and decided to begin with gratitude.

"I put Psalm 32:8 at the top of the paper which says, *'I will instruct you and teach you in the way you should go'* and then I wrote over two pages of things that I was grateful for... whatever came to my mind."

After she listed everything that was on her heart to say thank you for, she received a divine download with specific instructions on who she was to serve in her business, as well as the solutions she would provide for them. It was a shift in her business and an answer to her prayers.

It was a business meeting with God that lasted less than an hour, with the majority of the time spent on gratitude, and 5 minutes capturing divine strategy. "In the past, I would sit and wait for instructions, but what I learned is that while you're waiting for strategy and plans, simply say *thank you!*"

Tiffany recognizes that not every business meeting with God yields the same type of divine downloads; however, she maintains a heart of expectation, knowing that whatever God speaks, will be precisely what the moment required.

For me, I don't have one specific routine or length of time when I meet with God. My business meetings may be full of praise and gratitude with worship music playing softly in the background.

Other times it's asking specifically for wisdom and clarity concerning opportunities that lie before me and decisions that need to be made. Sometimes it's primarily prayer regarding the people I serve, my team, and specific people that the Lord places on my heart.

I often journal, meditate on scriptures, declare His promises, or simply fix my thoughts on Him. My business meetings are a combination of some or all of the above!

The beauty of doing business in partnership with God is that you can conduct meetings whenever you want and as often as you'd like. He's always available, never late, and always right on time! Remember that flowing supernaturally in your business happens when you keep company with Jesus, so don't feel as though you're boxed into a once per day meeting with God.

Keep the conversation going throughout your work days, plus have a personal Sabbath regularly when you unplug, and the only business-related activity you conduct is spending time with God.

Make Plans But Be Flexible

Proverbs 16:1-3 says, "The preparations of the heart *belong* to man, But the answer of the tongue *is* from the LORD. All the ways of a man *are* pure in his own eyes, but the LORD weighs the spirits. Commit your works to the Lord, and your thoughts will be established."

What the scripture is saying is that you have freedom of thought and free will to make plans, but the answer (the reply and the success) lies in God's response to those plans. He can and often does guide, change, and redirect them, so it's important to have an ear to hear and be flexible.

Commit (transfer the burdens of) your business activities to the Lord and trust Him with them. When you do that the Bible says that your thoughts (intention, imagination, and plans) will be established (or fixed, ordained, and perfected) by God. You will have the mind of Christ and be

in alignment with His will for your business --
there's no better place to be!

I cannot overemphasize the power of
embracing your freedom of thought. Too often
Kingdom Driven Entrepreneurs get stuck in over-
analysis and fear (the "grinding in your mind")
due to concerns regarding whether the plans on
their hearts are in God's will.

The Bible tells us in Psalm 37:4 that when you
delight yourself in the Lord, He will give you the
desires of your heart. This scripture is often
misunderstood to mean that God will give you
whatever you want, but that's not what it means
at all.

Let's do a quick Bible study:

If you study the Hebrew root of the word
delight, it is `anag which means to be delicate
and pliable. The word give is the Hebrew root
nathan which translates to several words
including set, put-upon, assign, and designate.
The word desires is *mish'alah* which means
request and petition.

With this insight, you can see that Psalm 34:7
means that when you're delicate and pliable in

your relationship with the Lord, He will place (put upon you) the very secret petitions and prayers on your heart.

This heart revelation is so important, because when you understand that God has placed those petitions and prayers on your heart, then you realize that your thoughts are aligned with His will, and you can move forward boldly in faith; making adjustments as needed along the way.

Be Diligent with a Spirit of Expectancy

Working in God's rest does not mean sitting around doing nothing. As James 2:17 indicates, your faith without any corresponding action is useless.

To be clear, I'm not talking about grinding. However I am talking about being thoughtful, prayerful, and consistent about your work.

Those plans you've submitted to God? Those ideas you have on your heart? Those instructions that you've received? Well, you'll need to do something with them and while you're at it

expect God to breathe on those plans and do
what only He can do.

Ask and expect to receive divine downloads,
strategic direction, and godly wisdom. When
you're working in His rest, everything that flows
from your business is a result of Christ working
in you.

If you've had an idea resting in your heart for
a while and it begins to show up in your thoughts
again or in your dreams at night, get engaged!

Reject timidity, accept the spirit of boldness
that resides on the inside of you, and get to work.
Prayerfully take consistent steps in the direction
of that idea so that you can get positioned for
what God has for you.

Diligence isn't only needed to move from little
to no action to consistent action; it is also needed
to move from complacency to bolder action.

There are too many God-given dreams that
stall and die in comfort and complacency zones.
Those dreams will come alive (and so will you)
when you take faithful action to make bolder
moves in your business while resting in the
goodness, provision, and faithfulness of God.

Think About What You're Thinking About

It's important to renew your mind daily, and one of the ways to do that is think about what you're thinking about and align your thoughts with God's word. A great way of doing this is to use Philippians 4:8-9 as a filter. The scripture says *whatever is true, whatever is noble, whatever is right, whatever is pure, whatever is lovely, whatever is admirable, if anything is excellent or praiseworthy* -- think about such things.

Take your thoughts through the filter. Does it pass? Is it true? Do your thoughts reflect God's thoughts? Sometimes you'll know the answer by getting in the scriptures and allowing Holy Spirit to illuminate the word in your heart. Other times Holy Spirit will bring the word to you.

If the thought doesn't pass the filters, don't go off running full steam ahead with that thought; bring it captive. Make it a prisoner and turn it over to God, asking Him to replace it with His thoughts.

Embrace Sweet Sleep

Team No Sleep is not the team that you want to play on if you desire to experience God's best in your business. Instead, you want to enjoy His presence and His blessing of wisdom at night as you sleep.

Let's look at Proverbs 3:21-24:

> "My son, let them not depart from your eyes - keep sound wisdom and discretion; So they will be life to your soul and grace to your neck. Then you will walk safely in your way, and your foot will not stumble. When you lie down, you will not be afraid; Yes, you will lie down and your sleep will be sweet."

Now let's look at Psalm 127:2: "It is vain for you to rise up early, to sit up late, to eat the bread of sorrows; for so He gives His beloved sleep."

What you see through these scriptures is that following the wisdom of God found in His word and by His Spirit leads to sweet sleep and that it is useless -- even deceptive -- to be working non-stop on your business without getting sleep.

It doesn't matter if the reason you are not sleeping is because you're passionate about the work you're doing, or it is because you are stressed by the cares of life or complications in your business.

Either way, not sleeping means not accessing the blessing that you as God's beloved, receive by His grace during the night.

There are numerous times when I've asked God for a solution before going to sleep, and either had a dream or woke up the next morning with a fresh insight from Holy Spirit. I've had dreams revealing strategies and blueprints for the work we do with Kingdom Driven Entrepreneur as a ministry and business.

I'm reminded of the story of my friend and founder of MIG Soap & Body Company Jaime Cross, who left her corporate banking career behind to stay at home with her newborn and asked God to show her a billion-dollar idea that would allow her to serve people and provide for her family.

It was through a dream two weeks later that God showed her a business plan and then by His grace gave her the ability to consume and process a great volume of scientific information (completely foreign to her) to create natural healing products. Today she has a thriving business that is rapidly growing in both impact and profitability.

Believe and expect that God will impart divine strategies, solutions, creative ideas, and prophetic dreams while you're being refreshed and restored through sleep. Expect to receive divine counsel from Holy Spirit.

This is the heart of your Ultimate CEO and business partner concerning you.

Ask, and you will receive.

Wholly Reject Anxiety

Anxiety is not a fruit of the spirit and is not your portion. In order to stay working in the flow of the Spirit, when anxiety comes regarding something that is happening (or perhaps not happening) in your business, stop what you're doing. Your remedy for that moment is found in Psalm 46:10 where it says "Be still and know that I am God."

In the Passion Translation it says:

> *Surrender your anxiety!*
> *Be silent and stop your striving*
> *and you will see that I am God.*
> *I am the God above all the nations, and*
> *I will be exalted throughout the whole earth.*

Isn't that good? It says to be silent and stop your striving, and then you will see that I am God.

I love how my friend Andy Mason (author of *God With You At Work*) speaks about anxiety. He says "Anxiety is evidence of an inferior Kingdom. It's an invitation to greater intimacy with God."

I can tell you from personal experience that this works. I accept His invitation for greater intimacy in the moment, and I get silent so that I can see. Once I do that, then I can access His wisdom and/or move on to the next thing that needs to be done.

It's a beautiful and empowering thing to partner with Abba who loves me without measure, knows my end from the beginning and has promised to work all things together for good. You also have access to the peace of God by taking any matters that cause you anxiety to prayer.

One of my favorite scriptures is Philippians 4:6-7 which states *"Do not be anxious about anything, but in every situation, by prayer and petition, with thanksgiving, present your requests to God. And the peace of God, which transcends all understanding, will guard your hearts and your minds in Christ Jesus."*

These are promises from God. They are yours.

APPLICATION: ASK HOLY SPIRIT

Take a moment and ask Holy Spirit the following questions and then write down the answers you receive:

Which of these guiding principles do I need to focus on so that I can enjoy the unforced rhythms of Your grace as I work? What is the next immediate step or change that I need to take concerning this?

TESTIMONY:

Confessions of a Redeemed Workaholic

One of my friends, Shelley Hitz, is a prolific author and accomplished business owner with a heart for Kingdom advancement through the work she does in the marketplace. Here is her story of how she has embraced working by God's grace over her grind:

I am a redeemed workaholic. I've known it for years and yet couldn't break free. I tried behavioral modification, I tried setting boundaries, I tried so many "strategies."

However, it would only last for a while and then I'd be back where I was again. I finally hit the proverbial wall, and so I did something drastic. I took a five-week vacation from my business with the last seven days in a technology detox.

For the first time in my life I completely unplugged from my computer and phone - no email, texting, or social media. I found out that the world will not fall apart if I take a few days away. I thought I was indispensable and couldn't truly take time away from email and my business responsibilities on social media.

God showed me I could.

I set a vacation responder on my email, and my virtual assistant emailed my husband with one urgent request that I needed to reply to the entire week. Other than that, my team took care of moderating my Facebook group for Author Audience Academy, and I communicated with my members that I would be offline for one week. Sometimes what seems impossible is possible.

Without the ability to text or spending time on social media, I began to learn to talk constantly to the Lord instead. Similar to how the Bible says to pray continually. However, my prayer life had shrunk to just certain times of the day instead of a flow of conversation between my Papa (Father God) and me.

I've always been driven and have felt an urgency that work needs to be done NOW. God showed me previously that the voice driving me wasn't from Him, but was the enemy. During my seven-day technology detox, He gave me a name for it and so much more insight into it.

It's my "inner slave driver" and is what has driven me to workaholism and to try to prove myself to others for years.

But now... I'm more self-aware.

I'm feeling and processing my emotions instead of numbing them with a "quick fix" from social media or the internet. I'm hearing from the Lord in a deeper way again.

During my detox, I received more insight and heard more from the Lord than I did in the previous 6-12 months. I created space and put myself in a position to receive.

I'm overall much more observant of my environment. I take things in and see things I never saw before. Observation is a skill that is needed for creativity, especially my art, and so this will be of use to me in so many ways.

I have more hunger for the Word and prayer; feeling more at peace than I have for years. The muddy river water in my jar had time to settle, and now I have clarity and peace. It also feels as if a fog has been lifted from my brain.

I've begun praying again for divine appointments and looking for them. The Lord is using me in face to face relationships, and I've been praying with people on the spot for difficult things they shared with me.

They are left encouraged, but so am I.

My encouragement? Find time away from technology for true silence and solitude. Start practicing the Sabbath so that you have one day

40 | P a g e

per week to unplug and allow God to restore your soul.

I've been a Christian for over 25 years and am now just admitting that I had never truly practiced the Sabbath until now. I'm not sure why it took me so long, but I'm thankful to be in this new season of my life.

I am FREE.

Enjoy Your Relationship

These guiding principles will help you avoid making an idol out of hard work and mistaking your identity as being in your work or your achievements versus in Jesus Christ. When you apply them, you won't allow grinding to make you miss out on God ideas, inspired thoughts, divine downloads, warnings, and course corrections which are all gifts of God's empowering grace.

Partnering with the supernatural flow of God and in His rest looks quite different from the world's way of entrepreneurship and even the way of many Christians in business, but it is His best.

Above all else, enjoy your relationship with God and never leave intimacy with Him behind in order to pursue the vision that He placed on your heart. Not only is God your Ultimate CEO and your business partner, but He is also your friend. He says in His word to draw near to Him, and He'll draw near to you. He says He reveals His secrets to you because you're His friend. He's gone into your future and prepared a way for you.

Talk to Him and often. Listen to Him. Stay aware of Him. Dream with Him. Enjoy the relationship because the more you spend time with Him and yield to Him, the more you'll look like Him and carry His heart to the world around you.

3

DIVINE FAVOR

Divine (or supernatural) favor is a demonstration of God's sovereignty and loving-kindness towards His children.

It is a manifestation of blessing that is designed to help you and to help others extend the Kingdom of God on earth; an amazing benefit of working by God's grace.

The favor of God yields both material and spiritual benefits. It brings influence, divine appointments, divine connections, promotion, unusual preferential treatment from people, sudden breakthroughs, financial provision, redemption from missed opportunities; all of which you could not have done on your own, and all of which will ultimately glorify God in the eyes of others, and draw you into closer relationship with Him.

With divine favor, things that would have taken you ten years to do in your business will be accomplished within months. You'll find yourself sitting in key meetings that you normally would not have the credentials to be invited to. Things that would have otherwise been impossible are suddenly made possible.

You absolutely need the favor of God (and the favor of men that He orchestrates) in order to accomplish the dreams He has placed in your heart for the marketplace.

Consider the story of Esther. The favor of God made this young Jewish woman the Queen of Persia during a time when there was a massive plot to destroy all the Jews. The favor she received from God, and the favor He orchestrated on her behalf with men (she obtained favor in the sight of ALL who saw her), combined with her humility, courage, and faith placed her in a position to protect her people from genocide.

Consider the story of Moses and the children of Israel. God gave them favor in the sight of the Egyptians, and when the Israelites did as Moses instructed and asked the Egyptians for gold, silver, and clothing before leaving Egypt, the Egyptians willingly gave them what they asked for, and they left with great wealth.

Consider the story of Joseph. He was sold into slavery by his begrudged brothers, but the favor of God caused him to prosper in the house of his master Potiphar. The Bible says that Joseph was successful in all that he did and when Potiphar saw this, he put him in charge of his entire household, and his household was blessed.

Not only that, but when Joseph later ended up in prison, God gave him favor with the prison warden, and through his God-given ability to interpret dreams, he lands in Pharaoh's palace.

The story continues, and throughout it all, God's favor and loving-kindness is evident... not just to Joseph individually, but also to those within the sphere of influence in which God placed him.

How about Jesus Christ? The Bible says in Luke 2:52 that Jesus himself increased in favor with God and with men (more on that soon).

When God places you in a favored position, He gives you influence in order to be a blessing to the people around you.

You are blessed (empowered to prosper) in order to be a blessing to others.

It is certainly possible to earn the favor of men and gain influence in your own strength. In fact, Dale Carnegie's *How to Win Friends and Influence People* is one of the best-selling self-help books of all time and has been read by millions of entrepreneurs around the globe, since it was published in the 1930's. It is full of insights and principles that will increase your favor and influence with people.

These are good practices, but too many entrepreneurs stop with the natural favor that must be earned. The invitation God is offering you is to ignite a confident expectation for something distinctively more powerful than natural favor that is earned and maintained on your own.

He is inviting you to experience divine favor in your business; favor that is orchestrated by Him.

Receiving Divine Favor

When it comes to receiving God's favor there is a strong element of God's sovereignty involved; He can do whatever He wants, for whomever He wants, and at whatever time He desires to do it.

You don't receive it because you're so awesome, but because God is! However, you're most likely to see divine favor manifest in your life when you're aligned with His purposes. The Bible gives us insight on how we receive favor in the sight of God.

1. By living a life of mercy and truth according to Proverbs 3:4

*"Let not mercy and truth forsake you;
Bind them around your neck, Write them on the
tablet of your heart, And so find favor and high
esteem in the sight of God and man."*

What does it mean to bind these around your neck and write them on your heart?

GRACE OVER GRIND

It means allowing these qualities to be the attitude of your heart and expressing them through your actions to the people around you, including those you encounter through the work that you do in the marketplace. It means to allow Holy Spirit to change you into God's image as you grow in the knowledge of who He is.

When you do this, you win favor and a good name in the sight of God.

2. By walking with Him blamelessly according to Psalm 84:11

*"For the Lord God is a sun
and shield; the Lord bestows favor
and honor; no good thing does he withhold
from those whose walk is blameless."*

You may think that sounds impossible, and you wouldn't be alone in that thinking. I had a similar reaction when I initially read this scripture and knew I was going to need to dig deeper to understand what this meant and how to practically apply it in my life and business.

The Hebrew word for blameless is *tâmîym* and it means upright, complete, without blemish, and perfect. By looking at some of the other scriptures that use this same Hebrew word (namely Joshua 24:14, Judges 9:16, Judges 9:19, Proverbs 11:5), we can get a better understanding about what it looks like to walk blameless before God.

Walking blamelessly means serving, both God and others, in sincerity and truth. This is possible because God makes our way perfect, by arming us with strength (Psalm 18:32) and the power of Holy Spirit, so that we have everything we need for life and godliness (2 Peter 1:3).

3. **By listening to and heeding God's instructions according to Proverbs 8:33-35**

"Listen to my instruction and be wise; do not disregard it. Blessed are those who listen to me, watching daily at my doors, waiting at my doorway. For those who find me find life and receive favor from the Lord."

God is releasing favor, opening doors and elevating people who have accepted the call to minister not just in words, but through their day to day living and working.

He is seeking entrepreneurs who dream with Him and whose hearts genuinely seek after Him.

TESTIMONY:
The Bakery That Jesus Built

I love the story of my friend Alicia Boyea Hommon, owner-operator of *The Laughing Place Bakery* in Gladstone, Missouri.

Her transition from a home-based bakery to the storefront bakery of her dreams, completely debt-free, is an amazing testimony of God's supernatural favor.

While most business owners who build out a physical store location do so with business loans, Alicia wanted to experience God's best by standing in faith to grow her business without any debt. Here's her story, which she shared in the book *The Kingdom Driven Entrepreneur's Guide to Debt Free Business:*

I can personally attest to the fact that God prepares a way for us if we only allow Him to. He will grant favor in places where there is no explanation for favor; where we do not even deserve it. When working with the city council of the community I built the bakery in, I was up against three other businesses for the opportunity to be given the lease for the space.

Though I was bringing in nothing financially to the venture, and the other businesses undoubtedly were bringing financing and small business loans to the table, God gave me favor with those making the decision, and ultimately I was given the lease.

Later on in the process, while meeting with a representative from the city and the architect who had created a design for the build out of my space, I had yet another miraculous moment of favor and grace.

In order to get the storefront for my bakery, I had to make several proposals to the city council that would ultimately be my landlord. When we first started the process of showing them why we were the best choice for them, my husband and I had $6,000 set aside from a bonus he had received from work. Even now, $6,000 might as well be $6 million for us, so this was a very big deal. We just knew God had given us this blessing to build His bakery.

I went through several rounds of proposals, amazed that we had made it through each one, knowing full well the other candidates were bringing much more money to the table; willing to take on business loans to bring their visions to life. At one point, I was two days away from having to sit down at a table with the architect I had worked with to design my space and a representative for the city.

This was a meeting that would determine the cost needed to build my vision and would give me an opportunity to say *yes*, I want to continue in the process; or *no*, this isn't for me.

Personally, I was looking at our situation and railing at God a bit. *"I don't understand what is going on here, God! Everything is falling apart. Two vehicles and a lawnmower need to be fixed. I need new glasses, the girls need clothes, the baby needs diapers, and bills still haven't been* *paid. All because I've been saving this $6,000 for a store that might never happen. I trust you, God, but what do I do?"*

Do you know what He said to me? *"Baby girl, I never said that money was for your store. Let today's troubles be sufficient for today."*

I'm sure you can imagine the fear I felt when I sat at my kitchen table, bills spread before me, to take care of what was falling apart in my life at the time. I paid my bills, thinking I would only spend $1,000, but by the end of that day, I had spent every penny of that $6,000.

I had nothing left and was going to have to sit in front of a representative of the city and tell her there was nothing left of the funds I had so confidently told her I would be contributing.

I walked into that meeting the next day confident I had done the right thing. I was full of faith that God would do with me exactly as He had planned (He certainly wasn't surprised I didn't have a penny left), but I was quaking in the knees for what I was about to do.

I sat down at the table. I listened as the architect laid out the cost of my space. In my do-it-yourself, working on my home naivety, I did not know my $6,000, now gone, would have been barely a drop in the bucket of the true cost of building a commercial space!

My heart sank to the bottom of my belly. *"Ok, God. It was always Yours anyway... take it if You must."*

I turned to the city representative, and before I could speak a word of my current situation, she proceeded to lay out a plan of how this space could be built; a plan that included a timeline that gave me the opportunity to utter a resounding "YES!" to her next question, *"Are you still interested in moving forward in the selection process?"*

Friends, I never had the opportunity to tell her that I no longer had the $6,000 I had promised. It was all I could do to walk out of that meeting before the tears began to pour down my face. When I tell you God is faithful to the vision He has given you, I mean it.

I live it... daily.

TESTIMONY:

God Hits the Pause Button

Another fun and compelling testimony from Alicia demonstrates how God's favor will supernaturally redeem missed opportunities. She wrote me the following message just weeks before her opening day of *The Laughing Place Bakery*:

I was given, free of charge, a $3000 Hobart mixer. It had no bowl or attachments. I was so excited, because I figured I could find a bowl and attachments, and do some minor repairs, and be in for $500 or less. Mind you; I am earthly penniless.

But Jesus.

I found a bowl on an auction a few days ago and placed a bid. I was instantly outbid, but something told me to wait until right before the auction closed to place another bid.

Fast forward to tonight. The auction was set to close at 7:30 PM Central Time.

I worked all day, and then we moved equipment into the store all evening. I walked in the door at 7:40 PM Central Time. Startled and devastated, I realized I had missed the end of the auction.

For some reason, (glutton for punishment, I guess), I went online to see how much I had lost the bowl for. This bowl would cost me $410 new. As I got online, I saw the red countdown numbers. Somehow, (Jesus) there are 14 minutes left.

I kid you not... Jesus stopped time for me. I made a bid and watched as those 14 minutes counted down; constantly refreshing the screen. When the auction ended at 7:30 PM Central, my phone, iPad, and house clocks all said 7:54 PM.

I am the proud new owner of a $410 Hobart bowl for which I paid just $17.50.

APPLICATION: DREAM WITH GOD

Take 30 minutes to dream with God regarding your business.

What are some things you desire to see happen in or through your business that will require divine favor in order to happen?

Increasing in Divine Favor

Earlier I mentioned that Jesus Christ himself increased in favor with God and with men; according to 1 Samuel 2:26, Samuel did as well.

I believe this is important to note because it means that everyone is given a measure of favor and that the measure can be increased; all of this made possible because of the grace of God on our lives. So, how can you increase in favor, working by God's grace instead of your grind?

In the Parable of the Talents, Jesus illustrated the power of proper stewardship; faithfulness over what we've been given makes us rulers over more. This same principle applies to the measure of favor you're given. The first step is that you must accept the favor God has given you.

This may sound ridiculous, but it needs to be said, because not everyone does. Some people refuse the favor that God has granted to them because they don't feel worthy of it. Favor isn't all about you and has nothing to do with your worthiness; it's about the assignment God has placed on your life. Remember that God uses imperfect and unlikely people to accomplish extraordinary things. All He needs is a surrendered and willing heart.

Not only must you accept the measure of favor that God has given you, but you have to do something *with it* in order to see it increase. When God opens the door for you, walk through it and continue seeking His face as you navigate.

Did God clear the way and open a door for you to have a meeting with someone who could accelerate what you're doing in business? Be sure to prepare for the meeting and be on time (early)!

Did Holy Spirit prompt you to submit a bid proposal on a project that seems like it would be impossible to get?

Submit the proposal!

It's so important to come in agreement with the favor that you've been given and steward it with a spirit of gratitude and expectation. When you do, watch your favor increase!

God's increasing favor does not only apply to things that you need in your business, but also the desires of your heart. You may not *need* to have the top of the line audio equipment you've had your eye on for your media production or the best ergonomic chairs for you and your clients to sit in your office, but God in His goodness delights in making it possible for you to have it anyway.

In the early days of Kingdom Driven LLC, my daughter accidentally spilled an entire glass of water on my MacBook and damaged it beyond repair. There's never a good time to have a $1,200 laptop ruined, but the timing was definitely not ideal, and the finances were not available to replace it, as I'd stopped my previous business activities to focus on the work of Kingdom Driven Entrepreneur that God assigned to me.

I could have purchased a new laptop for a few hundred dollars, but my heart's desire was to replace it with another MacBook. I asked God for a solution, and He gave me the name of a friend and fellow business owner. He told me if I asked her to purchase a MacBook for me, she would be honored to do it. He specifically instructed me to simply ask without providing all the details for why I was asking.

Can I be honest with you? I was sick to my stomach at the idea of asking her to make such a significant purchase for me. What would she think of me when I asked?

It was pride.

I recognized it as such, and after shedding plenty of tears, I made the phone call anyway. God opened the door and not only did this friend say yes immediately without question, but she thanked me for the opportunity to do it and gave me the option to choose any model of the MacBook I wanted.

Thanks to God's grace and my friend's generosity, a brand new MacBook Pro arrived on my doorstep three days later.

Not only was my laptop replaced, but it was upgraded because God is so good and I was willing to push past false humility (self-centered pride) and steward the favor that God had blessed me with.

APPLICATION: ASK HOLY SPIRIT

Take a moment and ask Holy Spirit the following question and then write down the answer you receive:

Am I properly stewarding the favor you have given me? If not, what are the next steps I should take in order to come in agreement with the measure of favor You've given me?

God's Favor and Promotion vs. Self-Promotion in Business

Part of working by God's grace, instead of your grind, is recognizing that God is your #1 promoter and you don't need to elevate yourself.

Sure, you can force things by grinding it out, and it can lead to promotion, elevation, and increase; however, experiencing God's best means allowing promotion to come from the Lord and His timing. What you force through your grind to create, you will have to maintain yourself. This easily leads to stress, pride, and destruction across multiple areas of your life.

God gets no glory from that, and you delay (or even worse forfeit) His best, which exceeds all you can ever ask, think, or even imagine!

On the other hand, where God gives favor and promotes you, He will sustain you. Not only that, but God will shine the light and compel others to get involved in your prosperity. Your job is to work in excellence and diligence as unto the Lord, sowing seeds as you're led. Those are seeds sown, and they will reap a harvest.

He will promote you, and He will also increase your income.

What we know from the scriptures is:

- To exalt means to elevate or lift up
- God is the Judge and is the one who exalts us (Psalm 75:6-7)
- Whoever exalts himself will be humbled, but whoever humbles himself will be exalted (Matthew 23:12)
- God has a proper time and season, a "due time" when He exalts the humble (1 Peter 5:5-7)

I'm not saying that you shouldn't plant seeds for opportunities that will yield visibility for yourself or your business. I'm also not saying that you shouldn't share about who you are, how you serve, and how others have benefited from the products and services you offer.

What I am saying is that while you're diligent in doing what you do in business, serving others to the glory of God, and partnering with Him, you are going to be prepared and positioned for a God-kind of promotion. He will present opportunities, grant you favor, increase you, open doors that no man can shut, and hand you the keys!

You don't have to chase after contracts with clients that are not aligned with your values simply because that client will look good for your portfolio and elevate you in the eyes of others.

You don't need to publicly or privately trash your competition so that your business looks better. Nor, do you have to be open for business seven days a week to be competitive in your industry when God is leading you to be open for fewer days. Chick-Fil-A generates more revenue per restaurant than any fast-food chain and is closed on Sunday in order to honor God and family.

Whenever you're feeling the urge to force things, rather than flow with God, remember that you've been given the solution of how to deal with it. Humble yourself under the mighty power of God, giving all of your worries and cares to Him. When you do, He will promote you and increase your territory and influence in His perfect timing (which is always better than your timing).

Expect to experience divine favor in your business. The heart of God is to see the Kingdom advanced through the marketplace; so that Jesus receives the inheritance of people and nations that He sacrificed His life for.

He will stop at nothing to ensure that those courageous enough to walk into the deep waters and partner with Him have access to Heaven's resources to accomplish this mission.

4

THE SUFFICIENCY OF GRACE

Working by God's grace does not mean that you will escape challenges. You will undoubtedly experience trials and undesirable circumstances in your business, but this is where grace meets you. Grace is the empowerment that enables you to successfully do what God has called you to do.

Not only does this grace offer you a lifestyle of unforced rhythm, rest, and divine favor, but according to God, His grace offers the solution to difficulties you will face on your entrepreneurial journey.

In 2 Corinthians 12:8-9, the Apostle Paul shared that when he pleaded with God and asked Him three times to take away the thorn in his flesh, God's response was *"My grace is sufficient for you, for my power is made perfect in weakness."* Paul goes on in verse 10 to describe some of the weaknesses he encountered; insults, hardships, persecutions, and difficulties.

God says that His transforming power is made complete in all of our weakness and that is extraordinary news.

I became intimately aware of this truth during my own journey, after my husband Phil and I had to sell our personal residence to avoid a foreclosure, in a season when the finances were strained. Neither of us had jobs, and we were new to this Holy Spirit-led journey of growing as a full-time entrepreneurial household.

Having to sell the house wasn't the hard part for us; in fact, there was an abundance of evidence that God's hand and His favor was upon each step we took during the short sale process. The problem was that we weren't sure where our (then) family of four was going to live next. We stayed in hotels for a few weeks, while we prayed about our next step, and searched for a place for our family.

One night I woke up and looked at the clock in the hotel room. It was a little after 1 a.m. The room suddenly seemed cramped, and I had difficulty breathing. I sat up in the bed, hoping to get my breathing under control, but instead, an intense surge of anxiety came over me. I nudged my husband to wake him and tell him what I was feeling. He instructed me to get dressed and said that we were going to leave the hotel room and go for a walk.

For the first time during this wild and crazy adventure with God, the circumstances surrounding me were completely overwhelming me. We left the hotel, and while the cool breeze was refreshing, it was still so hard to breathe. Phil was quiet and held my hand as he led the way during our walk. I was keenly aware that with each slow and deep breath, it was God breathing for me.

I had nothing left, but yet He had everything. Soon, I was able to breathe again; I was so appreciative that I began to sing.

The Lord your God in your midst, The Mighty One, will save; He will rejoice over you with gladness, He will quiet you with His love, He will rejoice over you with singing.
~Zephaniah 3:17 (NKJV)

Tears fell down my face as I felt my Father singing over me in response. At that moment, I knew that everything was going to be ok. I was deeply loved, fiercely protected, and very much provided for.

People often say that God doesn't give you more than you can handle, but the truth is that the journey of growing a Kingdom-driven business is way more than you could handle, yet nothing that He can't handle. Your ability to endure, persevere, and then thrive is the manifested fruit of God's grace that rests on your life. You will have peace in the midst of seeming chaos, and joy, in the midst of unfamiliar levels of hardship or criticism.

Others would crack under the pressure, give up and quit, but you don't because of that special grace to do what God has called you to do.

I once heard William Paul Young, author of the best-selling novel *The Shack* say "We have to learn how to live within the grace of one day only. We're designed to be the child, to live inside the grace of one day and deal with what's right in front of us. When you learn to do that, there will always be enough."

Read that again, pause for a moment, and let those words settle in your spirit. Live within the grace of one day only. That's how we experience the sufficiency of God's grace.

It truly is enough.

APPLICATION: ASK HOLY SPIRIT

Take a moment and ask Holy Spirit the following question and then write down the answer you receive:

What does living within the grace of one day only look like for me?

5

NOW WHAT?

If you grind long and hard enough, you will get results in your business. You can absolutely achieve business success by the world's standards in your own strength, requiring exertion and excessive hard work. You can even tell the world *"To God be the glory!"* in the process and give Jesus Christ credit for the outcomes of your own grind.

Alternatively, you can embrace the invitation laid before you to embrace a new standard, one that seeks God's best, testifies of His amazing grace, and ultimately has greater Kingdom impact.

It is time to make a decision with what Holy Spirit has revealed to you regarding your current approach to doing business, His best for you, and any gaps that exist between the two. Remember the words Holy Spirit shared with me: "Too many believers in business idolize hard work. They exalt hard work over the presence of God in business."

If that is how you've been operating your business, you can repent now. In other words, you can change your mind and change your actions. You're not too far off the beaten path. God is right there with you and eager to be involved and show you things that will astound you! Your business can serve as a sign and wonder, full of grace and power.

Not only can it serve as a sign to unbelievers, but also to believers that God is calling higher and into greater relationship with Him.

Making this decision to walk into deeper waters takes courage, but it is worth it. Prepare your heart to deal with naysayers (including brothers and sisters in Christ) that don't get it. There may even be business owners with financially thriving businesses that think you're crazy because this is not the way they achieved success.

You will also be inundated with messages that are contrary to those in this book, and you may even begin to think that others are right and you are indeed crazy!

I encourage you to stay the course and be sensitive to the leading of Holy Spirit.

Perhaps you are already working by God's grace instead of your grind, and this book primarily served as confirmation for you. If so, I want to encourage you to go even deeper and allow God to mature and grow you in grace.

2 Peter 1:2-3 says "May God give you more and more grace and peace as you grow in your knowledge of God and Jesus our Lord." Growing in knowledge comes from applying what you have heard and what you have seen from Holy Spirit, yielding undeniable testimonies and spiritual wisdom. As you grow in truly knowing Him, His grace will be multiplied to you.

Identify an area of development that will help you grow in intimacy with your Father; while partnering with His grace in greater ways in your business.

APPLICATION: ASK HOLY SPIRIT

Take a few minutes and ask Holy Spirit the following question and then write down the answer you receive:

How else can I use the information presented in this book and what You've revealed to me as I've read it to better serve You and others?

There is an entire sphere of influence awaiting you to release what God has placed on the inside of you. There is a world out there waiting on you and hungry for an encounter with God. I believe that there are days upon us that will require Kingdom-driven entrepreneurs to have solutions and a level of abundance that will only come from accessing the supernatural resources of Heaven.

The world is and will be seeking answers to seemingly impossible problems, and those answers will be found in the people who are completely yielded to God and resting in His grace rather than depending on their own strength.

Nothing will be impossible for you when your motives are pure, and your business pursuits are willingly surrendered to God. Raise your expectations, press into His presence, and remember that God is able to make all grace abound toward you, that you, always having all sufficiency in all things, may have an abundance for every good work (2 Corinthians 9:8).

God's grace will take your business where grinding can't.

APPLICATION EXERCISES

Chapter 1: God's Empowering Grace

#1: Ask Holy Spirit, "In what ways am I currently grinding in business and relying upon my own strength?" Record the answers you receive.

Chapter 2: Rhythm & Rest

#2: Ask Holy Spirit, "How can things be different in my business if I consistently partner with the supernatural flow provided to me by God's grace?" Record the answers you receive.

#3: Ask Holy Spirit, "Which of these guiding principles do I need to focus on so that I can enjoy the unforced rhythms of Your grace as I work? What is the next immediate step or change that I need to take concerning this?" Record the answers you receive.

Chapter 3: Divine Favor

#4: Take 30 minutes to dream with God regarding your business. What are some things you desire to see happen in or through your business that will require divine favor in order to happen?

#5: Ask Holy Spirit, "Am I properly stewarding the favor you have given me? If not, what are the next steps I should take in order to come in agreement with the measure of favor You've given me?" Record the answers you receive.

Chapter 4: The Sufficiency of Grace

#6: Ask Holy Spirit, "What does living within the grace of one day only look like for me?" Record the answers you receive.

Chapter 5: Now What?

#7: Ask Holy Spirit, "How else can I use the information presented in this book and what You've revealed to me as I've read it to better serve You and others?" Record the answers you receive.

A COMPANION JOURNAL

Dedicated to those who choose
to accept the invitation to live and work by God's grace
rather than by their grind.

Journal Sections

INTRODUCTION

This companion journal is designed to provide a guided journaling experience to help you process all that Holy Spirit speaks to you during and after reading *Grace Over Grind: How Grace Will Take Your Business Where Grinding Can't.*

Staring at a blank sheet of paper can be daunting at times, so my prayer is that the guided prompts provided in the following pages yield a transformative journaling experience.

How To Use This Journal

Holy Spirit abides in you and is your guide, teacher, comforter, and helper which is why several of the prompts instruct you to "Ask Holy Spirit." Use this journal as you read (and re-read) each chapter in *Grace Over Grind* and make the journaling a dedicated part of your quiet devotional time.

I encourage you to have a spirit of expectancy for God in all His fullness to reveal to you what you need in His perfect way and in His perfect timing.

I'm praising God in advance for the impact you will have for the Kingdom of God in the marketplace and the adventure you'll experience with Him which will be immeasurably more than all you can ask or imagine (according to His power that is at work within you)!

Shae Bynes
Your Chief Fire Igniter
Founder, Kingdom Driven Entrepreneur

God's Empowering Grace

Am I Grinding in My Business?

Grinding is working primarily in your own strength rather than allowing your work to flow from the empowering presence of God's grace. Some of the signs of include:

Financial Anxiety: You're feeling desperate about money or your thoughts are constantly consumed by how much money you are making (or not making) in your business.

Prayerlessness: Your prayers are infrequent or rushed or lack a sense of connectedness.

Lack of Sleep: You are experiencing habitual sleeplessness due to stress or excitement about the work you do. You're dissatisfied with the amount of time you have available to work.

Analysis Paralysis: You feel confused and overwhelmed and unable to move forward in your business due to frequent over-thinking and continuous analyzing.

No Boundaries: You make yourself available to your clients 24 hours a day, 7 days a week and keep your smartphone close at all times.

No Joy or Peace: You're tired, worn out, agitated, and carrying the stress of the everyday ups and downs of your business.

These are not the only signs; you may be aware of others that are signs for you. You may also be unaware of the signs of your grinding, but either way your heavenly Father knows!

Ask Holy Spirit, *"In what ways am I currently grinding in business and relying upon my own strength?"*

What did God speak to your heart or show you?

In all of the ways listed prior, and for years.

I realize after reading these books I am not praying enough, trusting enough, giving my plans over to good, not at all.

But the joy is, now the switch is flipped in my heart and I feel no worries. I'll keep praying...

Ask Holy Spirit *"What is the reason for my grinding? What's at the root of it?"*

Fear.

And it's honestly not believing God. Knowingly and unknowingly.

But looking back, He's always taken care of us.

And ya know how Elizabeth says we cockblock the universe? (horrible analogy i know) but that's what my fear, "control" and unbelief does for God.

↓ ↓ ↓ ↓
He wants to give me everything and I can't see it or accept it cause I'm in the way

Write out a prayer to your Father that expresses your desire for His help to address the root of your grinding.

God when I feel fear or anxious slap me in the face and remind me to let go and pray.

I know you will fulfill what I need.

You are faithful.

amen

Record anything that God speaks to you (either immediately or over time) in answer to your prayer.

GRACE GRIND

Rhythm and Rest

The Unforced Rhythms of Grace

Meditate on Matthew 11:28-30 in your favorite Bible translation as well as the Message Translation:

"Are you tired? Worn out? Burned out on religion?
Come to me. Get away with me and you'll recover your life.
I'll show you how to take a real rest. Walk with me and work
with me—watch how I do it. Learn the unforced rhythms of
grace. I won't lay anything heavy or ill-fitting on you. Keep
company with me and you'll learn to live freely and lightly."

Ask Holy Spirit, *"What do you want to show me through this passage?"*

tired, worn out, burned out
on religion ; that describes
most people. God can use
me as a tool to show
people that it doesn't have
to be that way. People
are missing out on Gods
Grace, ease, and uncond-
-itional love.

_____

_____

_____

_____

_____

_____

_____

_____

_____

_____

_____

_____

_____

_____

_____

_____

Keeping company, or abiding, with Jesus is the prerequisite for learning how to flow supernaturally in your business. The way to abide lies in intimacy with Him. It's keeping a line of two-way conversation going, allowing Him to speak to you through His Word, by Holy Spirit, and working from His rest.

Rest is an awareness of God's presence; it's simply something that you realize and access because you are one with Christ.

remain in me, I remain in you

Meditate on John 15:4 and Colossians 1:27 in your favorite Bible translation.

Christ in you, the hope of Glory?

Ask Holy Spirit, "What do you want to show me through these passages?"

I want to feel God's presence presence more than I can feel my anxiousness or emotions.

This requires me to actively exercise acknowledgement of His presence with me

Ask Holy Spirit, *"How can things be different in my business if I consistently partner with the supernatural flow provided to me by God's grace?"*

What did God speak to your heart or show you?

— ease
— no anxiety or worry
— Trust that it'll work
— It's not going to be all about me
— it will put my grace for others more on auto pilot..

Your Business Meetings with God

Giving God the first fruits of your day is a powerful way to work by His grace. If you don't already have a consistent time of meeting with God concerning your life and business, adjust your schedule to make room for it every day that you work.

Ask Holy Spirit, *"What should my daily business meetings look like with you?"* Create an agenda together and write about it below.

I need to do a meeting/quiet time with God at work.

In my office say a prayer and have some intentional time in my office before work.

I can do this at home too if I'm working at home that day.

What are the desires of your heart related to your business?

To coach/lead/minister to entrepreneurs like me struggling between worldly success, _____ and keeping God in the center of their plans, with Gods plan.

Technology Detox

Completely unplugging from your computer and phone for a period of time creates quiet space to hear from God, ignite new ideas, and be refreshed. Plan a technology detox.

What do you hope to experience during your detox?

Hearing Gods voice

What will you detox from and for how long?

_____

_____

_____

_____

_____

_____

_____

_____

What were the results of your time of unplugging?

_____

_____

_____

_____

_____

_____

_____

_____

_____

Ask Holy Spirit "How often should I unplug to create more space to delight myself in You?"

Working in Diligence

Working in God's rest does not mean sitting around doing nothing. As James 2:17 indicates, your faith without any corresponding action is useless. It's important to be thoughtful, prayerful, and consistent about your work.

Ask Holy Spirit, *"What have you given me to take action on that I have been resistant or slow to respond to?"*

----

104 | P a g e

What will be the next step you take to make progress and when will you begin?

_____

_____

_____

_____

_____

_____

_____

_____

What barriers, if any, do you need to overcome in order to make the next step?

_____

_____

_____

_____

_____

_____

Write out a prayer to your Father that expresses your desire for His help to address the barriers you need to overcome.

Record anything that God speaks to you (either immediately or over time) in answer to your prayer.

Think About What You're Thinking About

It's important to renew your mind daily, and one of the ways to do that is think about what you're thinking about, and align your thoughts with God's Word.

What are the promises you have from God concerning your business?

What are some of the recurring thoughts you have that are contrary to the word and promises of God concerning you?

Look in the scriptures and find the ones you will stand on when you have these thoughts. Write the scriptures below.

What other truths can you say to yourself in response to contrary and unproductive thoughts that show up?

Divine Favor

Receiving God's Favor

Divine (or supernatural) favor is a demonstration of God's sovereignty and loving kindness towards you. It is a manifestation of blessing that is designed to help you extend the Kingdom of God on earth and is an amazing benefit of working by God's grace.

The favor of God yields both material and spiritual benefits. It brings influence, divine appointments, divine connections, promotion, unusual preferential treatment from people, sudden breakthroughs, financial provision, redemption from missed opportunities; all of which you could not have done on your own and all of which will ultimately glorify God in the eyes of others and draw you into closer relationship with Him.

You're most likely to see divine favor manifest in your life when you're aligned with His purposes. You receive favor in the sight of God by:

- Living a life of mercy and truth according to Proverbs 3:4
- Walking with Him blamelessly according to Psalm 84:11
- Listening to and heeding God's instructions according to Proverbs 8:33-35

Meditate on each scripture mentioned above.
Ask Holy Spirit, *"What do you want to show me through these passages?"*

Ask Holy Spirit, *"Am I properly aligned with the purposes of God? What area do I need to develop more in?"*

Dream With God

Take 30 minutes to dream with God regarding your business.

What are some things you desire to see happen in or through your business that will require divine favor in order to happen? Be specific.

What are the possibilities for divine favor that you can imagine? What are some of the wild and amazing ways God can make these things happen? Take the limits off of your thinking here.

Stewarding the Favor of God

Not only must you accept the measure of favor that God has given you, but you have to do something with it in order to see it increase. It's important to come in agreement with the favor that you've been given and steward it with a spirit of gratitude and expectation.

When you do, watch your favor increase!

Write down every instance of favor that you can think of (both personal and business life) and thank God for it.

_____

_____

_____

_____

_____

_____

_____

_____

_____

_____

_____

Ask Holy Spirit, *"Am I properly stewarding the favor you have given me? If not, what are the next steps I should take in order to come in agreement with the measure of favor You've given me?"*

Ask Holy Spirit *"Is there any area where I have refused the favor of God?"* What did God speak to your heart or show you?

_____

_____

_____

_____

_____

_____

_____

_____

_____

If He showed you areas where you had or continue to have feelings of unworthiness, write a prayer to ask Him to help you address those areas of your heart.

_____

_____

_____

_____

_____
_____
_____
_____
_____
_____
_____
_____
_____
_____
_____

Record anything that God speaks to you (either immediately or over time) in answer to your prayer.

_____
_____
_____
_____
_____
_____

Experiencing God Promotions

Experiencing God's best means allowing promotion to come from the Lord and His timing. What you force through your grind to create, you will have to maintain yourself. This easily leads to stress, pride, and destruction across multiple areas of your life.

God gets no glory from that and you delay (or even worse forfeit) His best which exceeds all you can ever ask, think, or even imagine!

In what ways, if any, have you felt the urge to force things rather than flow with God?

_____

_____

_____

_____

_____

_____

_____

_____

_____

Ask Holy Spirit *"What do I still need to surrender to you as it relates to my business?"*

Write a prayer to express your heart to your Father concerning an increase of your territory, impact, and influence in the marketplace.

The Sufficiency of Grace

Grace in the Midst of Your Challenges

Your ability to endure, persevere, and then thrive is the manifested fruit of God's grace that rests on your life. You will have peace in the midst of seeming chaos and joy in the midst of unfamiliar levels of hardship or criticism.

Others would crack under the pressure, give up, and quit, but you don't because of that special grace to do what God has called you to do.

Write down some of the challenges you are currently experiencing in your business.

_____

_____

_____

_____

_____

_____

_____

_____

_____

_____

_____

Write a prayer in gratitude to God about His grace that rests on your life to help you overcome these challenges.

Ask Holy Spirit, *"What does living within the grace of one day only look like for me?"* **What did God speak to your heart or show you?**

Revelation from Holy Spirit

Ask Holy Spirit, *"How else can I grow in grace using the information presented in this book and what You've revealed to me to better serve You and others?"*

What did God speak to your heart or show you?

_____

_____

_____

_____

_____

_____

_____

_____

_____

_____

_____

_____

_____

_____

_____

Ask Holy Spirit *"How can I grow in intimacy with you?"* **What did God speak to your heart or show you?**

_____

Moving Forward

Making the decision to make a lifestyle of working by God's grace instead of your grind takes courage, but it is worth it!

Write a prayer to your Father to express your heart of surrender to His best for you and your business.

*And God is able to make
all grace abound toward you,
that you, always having all sufficiency in all
things, may have an abundance for every good
work.*

2 Corinthians 9:8

ABOUT THE AUTHOR

Shae Bynes is a passionate storyteller, teacher, and mentor whose life and business was completely transformed through the power of encountering the unrelenting love of God. Her heart is to see marketplace leaders and families that are courageous, connected, and aligned with Kingdom purpose.

Shae is the Founder and Chief Fire Igniter of *Kingdom Driven Entrepreneur* where she inspires, teaches, and mentors Christian entrepreneurs to be led by God in their businesses so they can experience His best and have a greater Kingdom impact in the marketplace.

Together with her husband and high school sweetheart Phil, Shae helps couples strengthen their marriages by cultivating true intimacy through the power and love of God.

Phil and Shae live in the Fort Lauderdale, Florida area with their three beautiful daughters.

ABOUT KINGDOM DRIVEN ENTREPRENEUR

God has a dream for individuals, families, communities, and industries and it requires sons and daughters in the marketplace who are discovering and aligning with their assignments.

Therefore, *Kingdom Driven Entrepreneur* exists to help Christian entrepreneurs experience God's best in business and have greater Kingdom impact in the marketplace.

We believe that nothing will be impossible when you partner with Him (The Ultimate CEO); this is why we inspire, teach, and mentor Christians called to entrepreneurship to be led by God in their business.

This isn't business as usual.

We invite you to join our community and enjoy the resources made available to you at:

KingdomDrivenEntrepreneur.com

OTHER BOOKS BY SHAE BYNES

The Kingdom Driven Entrepreneur: Doing
Business God's Way
(ISBN: 978-0615736129)

The Kingdom Driven Entrepreneur's Guide To
Goal Setting
(ISBN: 978-0615771892)

Encountering God: A Devotional for the Kingdom
Driven Entrepreneur
(ISBN: 978-0989632225)

The Firestarter Effect: Making Jesus Christ
Known in the Marketplace
(ISBN: 978-0989632256)

The Firestarter Effect: Activating the Power of
Covenant
(ISBN: 978-0-989632218)

Made in United States
North Haven, CT
29 December 2021

13825291R00085